# by Ellen Appelbaum
## illustrated by Alexandra Colombo

Harcourt
SCHOOL PUBLISHERS

ISBN 10: 0-15-351511-2
ISBN 13: 978-0-15-351511-8

Ordering Options
ISBN 10: 0-15-351213-X (Grade 3 Advanced Collection)
ISBN 13: 978-0-15-351213-1 (Grade 3 Advanced Collection)
ISBN 10: 0-15-358101-8 (package of 5)
ISBN 13: 978-0-15-358101-4 (package of 5)

3 4 5 6 7 8 9 10 985 12 11 10 09 08

Chester, the crow, flapped his wings wildly. He was attempting an emergency landing in the meadow. He had not been paying close attention, and he had almost flown past his destination. Chester had an important message to deliver. He straightened his feathers and soon recovered his balance. Then, adjusting his cap, he introduced himself to Willie, the pig, and Dillon, the mouse.

"How do you do," he began. "My name is Chester. Do either of you know a spider who goes by the name of Carla?"

"Yes, we all live on the same farm, and we are all very good friends," replied Dillon. "Why do you ask about Carla?" They were suddenly extremely interested and a little worried about what Chester had to say.

Chester cleared his throat and drew himself up to attention. "I have a message for you from Carla, the spider," he said with an air of importance.

"Yes, yes, do tell us!" exclaimed Dillon excitedly.

4

"Happy to oblige," said Chester. He removed a small, folded paper from his pocket, opened it up, and smoothed it flat. Then Chester cleared his throat and began to read in a scratchy voice.

Dear Willie and Dillon,

I am stuck in the hayloft at Oakley's Farm. I don't mean to be a nuisance, but I desperately need your help! Please come quickly.

Your friend,
Carla, the spider

Oakley's Farm was quite far away from the farm they all called home, but the weather had been quite windy the past few days—too windy for Carla to spin a web.

At first, Carla had tried to be patient. After three sedentary days of waiting for the weather to improve, though, Carla was hungry. She just had to spin a web. She let out a strand from her spinneret and took flight—and what a flight she took. The wind picked her up and blew her all the way to Oakley's Farm.

"The gusts of wind must have blown Carla off course," remarked Willie with a worried frown. "We must go and get her out of Oakley's hayloft!"

Willie and his friend, Dillon, had each just earned his pilot's license. For years, Willie had been boasting that he was "born to fly."

Today it was Willie's turn to fly. Dillon was the co-pilot, so his job would be to read the map and plot the best course for their journey. The two friends climbed into the cockpit of their two-passenger plane. Then they fastened their seat belts.

Dillon was cautious. His motto was, "You never know, so be prepared." He always had unexpected objects with him, such as the piece of string he had with him today. He would use the string to mark their route on the map.

Dillon unfolded the map and studied it carefully. "I have found the location of Oakley's Farm," he declared. "If we fly southwest for twelve miles, we will be there in just a few minutes. I've marked our course with string."

Willie started the engine and pressed on the gas pedal. The plane began to sway and then roll forward, slowly at first. Summoning more power and speed, it rolled faster and faster. Within moments, the plane was up in the sky.

"Whee!" shouted Willie.

"Hold on, let me check our position," hollered Dillon as he quickly placed the string at different points on the map. "You have to turn left, Willie." Willie turned the controls, and the plane headed left, on a southwesterly course.

Little by little, Oakley's Farm came into view on the left. Finally, Dillon said, "Prepare to land."

Dillon had paid so much attention to watching Willie land the plane that he had forgotten to concentrate on the map. A sharp gust of wind ripped it out of his hand, and it blew away!

"Uh-oh," murmured Dillon.

"Uh-oh," repeated Willie.

Dillon and Willie carefully guided their plane to a rolling stop in the meadow on Oakley's Farm. They were right next to the barn with the hayloft where Carla was stuck.

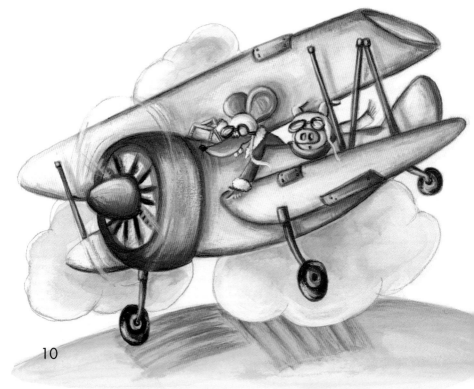

Now that they were safely on the ground, Dillon yanked off his goggles and leaped out of the plane. He began to clean his whiskers with his paws, which he always did when he was nervous. Willie climbed out of the cockpit extremely slowly. He waddled to a nearby patch of mud, and then he rolled and rolled and rolled in it.

"Hello, help, did I hear a plane? Is it Willie and Dillon?" Carla's voice called out from the barn. Dillon stopped grooming his whiskers, and Willie paused in his mud bath.

"Yes, we're here, Carla, is that you?" they exclaimed as they scrambled over to the barn.

Carla called out from inside a haystack that was next to the barn. "I declare, it's about time. Please hurry up and get this hay off of me. I'd never be able to spin a web inside a haystack, and after three days, I am so hungry I could eat a bear!"

"Well, Carla," Dillon smiled, "we have arrived to fly you home. We have our plane, you know."

"Well, we may have our plane, but we don't have our map," muttered Willie.

"I think I can be of some help to you there,"
cawed a voice behind them. Willie and Dillon
turned around, and there stood Chester, the crow.

"I was flying right behind you the whole way,
and I saw the map float away. You two were
paying so much attention to that map, going this
way and that, that you weren't even paying any
attention to where you were going. I will lead you
straight back home—as the crow flies."

"Willie, wake up, you're daydreaming again."

Willie shook his head from side to side as his ears flapped around gently. "Sorry," he muttered to Carla, the spider, who was scolding him in the barn.

"Were you dreaming about flying again?" demanded Carla. "I suppose you know the old saying *when pigs fly*. It means, 'Never in a million years!'"

"Well, Carla, we might just see about that," Willie said, with a mysterious grin.

# Think Critically

1. At the end of the story, Carla asks Willie if he is daydreaming again. What conclusion can you draw about Willie from this?

2. Find the map that Dillon drew on page 8. How can Dillon figure out the direction they have to fly to reach Oakley's Farm?

3. What does the saying *as the crow flies* mean?

4. Which character is the most helpful in this story? Explain.

5. Which character was your favorite? Why?

 **Science**

**Look it Up** Find a picture of a plane in a book and draw a picture of it. Label your picture with the names of some parts of the airplane you know.

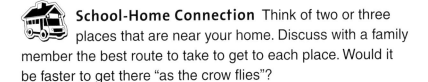 **School-Home Connection** Think of two or three places that are near your home. Discuss with a family member the best route to take to get to each place. Would it be faster to get there "as the crow flies"?